My Family and Other Families

Richard and Lewis Edwards-Middleton
Illustrated by Andy Passchier

The moment Liam has been looking forward to has arrived.

There is a funfair at the park and he is going to ride on the big wheel.

There's no time for food. No time for a coat.
The wheel won't wait!

The funfair has lots of different foods to try.

Who is that eating buttery popcorn?
It's Kajal and her grandparents.

Hi Liam!
My grandma and grandad
got me popcorn. I like a
mix of salty and sweet.
Would you like some?

What's that music?

Is that Oscar riding on the carousel with his dads?

Yeehaw Liam! Can you guess what

I've named my horse?

Liam did want to know what Oscar had named his horse.

But he had to get to the big wheel soon. After all, he had his ticket right...

Did Liam drop the ticket by Oscar's carousel?

There are three golden horses but no bright blue ticket.

Did the ticket fall out of Liam's pocket near Demi and her family?

There's one round wheel of fortune
but no bright blue ticket.

Everybody won prizes! Now the search can continue.

Is the ticket in a popcorn bucket? There's lots of buttery yellow popcorn but no bright blue ticket.

Did the ticket fall out of Liam's pocket at the tin can alley?

There's lots of colourful prizes.
One petal pink teddy.
One grass green owl.
One grizzled grey elephant.
One bright blue ticket–

It took Jack's mum...

...4

...9

...13 tries.
But she won the ticket!

We all worked together to save the day!
Not just one family, but other ones too.
Families are made in different ways.
A family is people who care about you.

About the Authors

Richard and Lewis live in London with their two children and love to document their family life through their social media accounts under the name Two Dads in London. Seeing how much their children enjoy and learn through story time inspired them to write a fun, imaginative picture book with an important message behind it: that every family is different and that is perfectly okay.

A note from Richard and Lewis

To Gemma, we will be forever grateful to you for making our dreams of a family come true.

About the Illustrator

Andy Passchier (they/them) is a non-binary illustrator from The Netherlands, currently based in the USA. Previous titles include *What Are Your Words?* By Katherine Locke, and *Being You* by Megan Madison and Jessica Ralli. Andy loves cats, videogames, Dungeons & Dragons, and shows about aliens.

Authors Richard and Lewis Edwards-Middleton
Illustrated by Andy Passchier

Editor Satu Hämeenaho-Fox
Project Art Editor Charlotte Bull
Inclusivity Consultant Lisa Davis
Production Editor Dragana Puvacic
Production Controller Leanne Burke
Publisher Francesca Young
Deputy Art Director Mabel Chan
Publishing Director Sarah Larter

First published in Great Britain in 2022 by
Dorling Kindersley Limited
DK, One Embassy Gardens, 8 Viaduct Gardens,
London, SW11 7BW

The authorised representative in the EEA is
Dorling Kindersley Verlag GmbH. Arnulfstr. 124,
80636 Munich, Germany

A CIP catalogue record for this book
is available from the British Library.
ISBN: 978-0-2415-6350-2

Printed and bound in China

For the curious
www.dk.com

FSC
www.fsc.org
MIX
Paper | Supporting
responsible forestry
FSC™ C018179

This book was made with Forest Stewardship Council™ certified paper – one small step in DK's commitment to a sustainable future. For more information go to www.dk.com/our-green-pledge